BREAKING FREE

• *The Story of William Kurelek* •

MAY EBBITT CUTLER • ART BY WILLIAM KURELEK

TUNDRA BOOKS

For Philip, Dylan, Sofia, Samantha, Chelsea, and Joey

Text copyright © 2002 by May Ebbitt Cutler
Illustrations copyright © William Kurelek Enterprises Limited 2002

Published in Canada by Tundra Books,
481 University Avenue, Toronto, Ontario M5G 2E9

Published in the United States by Tundra Books of Northern New York,
P.O. Box 1030, Plattsburgh, New York 12901

Library of Congress Control Number: 2002103704

National Library of Canada Cataloguing in Publication Data

Cutler, May, 1923-

    Breaking free : the story of William Kurelek / May Ebbitt Cutler ;
illustrations by William Kurelek.

ISBN 0-88776-617-X

    1. Kurelek, William, 1927-1977. 2. Painters–Canada–Biography.
I. Kurelek, William, 1927-1977. II. Title.

ND249.K87C84 2002   759.11   C2002-901396-8

We acknowledge the support of the Canada Council for the Arts and the Ontario Arts Council for our publishing program.

We acknowledge the financial support of the Government of Canada through the Book Publishing Industry Development Program for our publishing activities.

Printed in Hong Kong, China

1 2 3 4 5 6   07 06 05 04 03 02

"Forget your worries," Fox Mykyta said.
"Look at the beauty all around."

The village in the Ukraine where his father grew up was a place of misery. Armies fought back and forth over it in World War I, destroying the farms and killing the people. Those who survived faced starvation. His father was forced to leave school in grade three, when the building was taken over by Russian soldiers. He was nineteen when he left the Ukraine and came to Canada to work on a farm in Alberta, owned by another Ukrainian.

His father worked so hard that, when a romance developed between him and the daughter of the house, her father gave them a three-day wedding.

Then, as Bill would later write, "They loaded up their gifts in a wagon and drove off to their quarter of land. There, in a shacky little house, they spent their first night and were at work the next day on the land. I was born in that shack nearly two years later."

So began William Kurelek's unhappy childhood. The story of his life is how he broke free of it to become one of Canada's great artists.

His father could not have tried to farm in the West at a worse time. He got so little for the grain he sold, he could barely support his family. Desperate, he moved the family to a larger farm in Manitoba, where they would keep animals as well as work the land. But their luck did not change. The barn burned when it was full of hay. Then the milk house. One year, drought dried up the fields.

When World War II brought good prices for farm products, his father at last saw a chance to make good. He forced his sons to help. Bill was twelve and his brother John was eleven. They worked late into the night. "We tumbled into bed so tired we didn't even bother washing or changing. Yet the next morning we were expected to get up at 6:00 a.m. to fetch the cows for milking. . . . I still recall my pained numbed wrists after milking ten or twenty cows."

Yet he admired his father. When a swarm of grasshoppers destroyed the crop, "I recall him drawing the family together and saying, 'Never mind, we'll try one more year, and if it doesn't work, then I know of another farm east of here we can make a fresh start on.'

"That winter our diet consisted mostly of potatoes."

Sweeping hay could be dangerous if horses bolted from the flies. • *A Prairie Boy's Summer*

What hurt Bill most was not the work, hard as that was, but that he could never please his father. The more he tried, the more mistakes he made. "It seems," he wrote, "I was now bungling something or other every week, if not daily. I was painfully aware that with each slip I made, I was moving further and further from any possibility of closeness to my father. . . . I found myself on the verge of breaking into sobs whenever I was alone with him. It got so bad that the mere sound of my voice roused his contempt for my intelligence. . . . The terror of some as yet unknown physical punishment from him hung like the sword of Damocles over me."

Nighttime brought its own fears. Although he slept with his brother John, Bill hid under the bedclothes, imagining monsters were after him.

But no childhood, no matter how difficult, is without moments of happiness. In the two books he would write and illustrate about his prairie boyhood, he gave equal space to those good times: the excitement of helping his mother get the chickens inside when a thunderstorm threatened; the challenge of trying to carry fire from one pile of weeds to another when he burned quack grass; the fun of escaping to skinny-dip in the bog ditch.

You closed your eyes swimming in the muddy ditch, then ran around to dry off. • *A Prairie Boy's Summer*

School released him from daylong farm work, but there were still chores. Firewood had to be brought in, the snowcap over haystacks dug away to get at extra food for the animals, ice on water troughs broken so they could drink. When storms closed down the schools, Bill walked through blizzards to the chicken coup to gather eggs.

School meant other problems. Bill was shy, scrawny, and bullied by older boys. He was made fun of if he made mistakes speaking English. He was not good in sports. He helped build the hockey rink in the school yard, but he could not play well on skates. He was made goalie and played in his overshoes.

One kind of skating he did like. When the bog ditch froze over and the ice stretched for miles, he loved the "immense feeling of freedom" as he broke loose and skated toward the horizon. If he fell, he picked himself up and kept going – as he would in life.

As early as first grade, he made a discovery. He loved to draw. It was, he wrote, "the first sign I would become an artist. I noticed I could get admiration and, from all, a concession that I did excel in this one thing. Considering my failures in most every other activity at home and at school, it can be understood how the drive to create developed in me."

After every snowfall, the school rink had to be cleared and flooded. • *A Prairie Boy's Winter*

If there was anything Bill's father was more fanatical about than work, it was education. He used his savings to send Bill and John to Winnipeg to finish high school and go on to university. Bill wanted to be an artist. His father wanted him to be a doctor or a teacher.

Bill was nineteen and in his second year at college when he decided to spend a summer working in a lumber camp in Northern Ontario. "I did it," he wrote, "to prove to my father (and myself) that I could make it on my own. . . . My father was furious. His anger lasted until the very morning I was to leave. The day dawned overcast and chilly, to match the depression and guilt I felt about going against his wishes.

"I found the train and boarded it at sunset. I fully expected to fall into an even deeper depression, but immediately, to my surprise, my own sun came up." The work that summer was backbreaking but he loved the camaraderie, the storytelling, the huge meals, and the beauty of forests he'd never seen on the Prairies.

After university, he returned to the bush and worked like crazy in rain and snow, late into the winter. "After a heavy snowfall, it was disheartening to see a tree I had felled disappear from sight."

Bill needed the money. He had to get to England.

Hard work and fresh air gave us voracious appetites. • *Lumberjack*

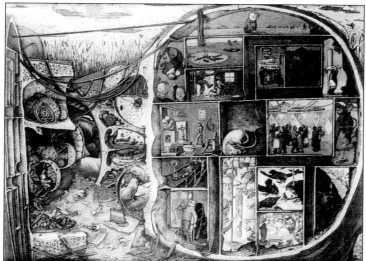

Bill wanted to get over the depressions that troubled him and he thought he was going blind. He had heard of a hospital in London that treated patients by encouraging them to draw or paint what they were afraid of.

His second day in England, he walked into that hospital. For the next three years, between hospital stays, he worked at temporary jobs. He also managed to get over to Europe to visit the great museums there. And he "learned to paint by painting."

In hospital he painted feverishly. In one famous work that would later be the basis of a prizewinning film, he showed the maze inside his head "depicting all my emotional problems." Two scenes were of "the father I hated and worshipped."

The English doctors were good to him, but the most help came from a motherly therapist. She was supposed to supply him with painting materials and encourage him to attend social gatherings. But she did more. She gave her own time to listen day after day as he poured out his bitterness. *How could she be so patient and kind?* he wondered. He found she, too, had known depressions. Her religion had helped her overcome them. So began his own religious search.

Two years later he became a Catholic. From that time, he wrote, "I am not really alone anymore in the rest of my journey through this tragic, puzzling, yet wonderful world. There is 'Someone with me.'" He set himself a monumental task to illustrate the Passion of Christ in one hundred and sixty paintings. He went to the Holy Land to retrace Jesus' steps.

Then he returned to Canada to stay.

Jesus preaching to his disciples in one of the *Passion of Christ* paintings. • *Niagara Falls Art Gallery*

Bill had come back to Canada once during his years in England, determined to forgive his father. His parents now lived on a small farm near Stoney Creek, Ontario and he found they, too, had changed. "Father greeted me at the Hamilton railway station with his first hug and a kiss. He was evidently emotionally overcome for they had nearly lost me." From then on, they would reach out to each other.

While in England, he had worked for a man who restored antiques. Working hard as usual, Bill soon became a master at gilding picture frames. It served him well. In Toronto, while he continued to paint, he got work in the framing shop of a leading gallery. When he brought in his paintings to show the owner, he was offered his first exhibition. It was an instant success.

"I had a distinct feeling of unreality standing there in the crowds," he later wrote. "It can't be my pictures all these people have come to see – must be someone else's. . . . To my big surprise, my parents actually had come to my first show and have been coming ever since."

A director of New York's Museum of Modern Art came to Toronto to choose works for its collection. A painting he selected was of an Alberta hailstorm and he asked to meet the artist. Bill said he'd take a streetcar and be there in an hour. They sent a taxi.

He would later paint an even more spectacular prairie storm. But something exciting in a very different way was happening.

Thunder Driven, in the rush to finish off a haystack before the full fury of a prairie storm. • *From a private collection*

Bill was in love.

They met at a religious center. He had got over his shyness enough to give talks about the faith that now meant so much to him. She was a nurse of English-Irish background, who worked as a volunteer helping street people.

He described her as "a smiling redhead whom I found myself turning to look at. She was not only smiling but beautiful. One winter evening she was leaving the center with her friends. I ventured to ask her, 'Say, what does it say on that notebook tag of yours?' She smiled and offered it. . . . I read 'Jean Andrews, Moore Avenue.' Less than a year later, I married Jean Andrews." He painted their honeymoon in Quebec City.

It was a good marriage. Jean was as open and calm as he was shy and intense. She would give him the help he needed when his depressions threatened to return. They would have four children. With Jean's help, he also learned to be a gentler father. They moved to a modest house in Toronto's east end, within walking distance of the beaches on Lake Ontario.

Enjoying an outing to the Toronto beach, just a few blocks from home. • *Kurelek's Canada*

Bill would have liked to paint only religious or "message" pictures, warning the world of disaster to come if it did not change its evil ways. He painted Jesus teaching from the steps of Toronto's city hall, with no one paying attention. It took him six years to complete his *Passion of Christ* paintings.

Of all his religious paintings, his dreams of the Nativity taking place across Canada were the most tender. "If it happened here and now," he asked, "who would take them in? Who would have even noticed the miracle?"

He painted the Holy Family finding shelter in the simplest places – in a night watchman's shack, in a gasoline station, in a freight car, on a fishing boat, at a lumber camp, in a grain elevator. He imagined Jesus born to an Inuit mother in an igloo, to a Native mother, as a black baby.

Who would have noticed? The cowboys rounding up cattle and anxious to get in from the cold – would they have realized what had happened in their barn that Christmas morning?

Bill painted himself into that scene as a little boy looking in, as he would in other paintings.

Was he the only one to see into the cowboys' barn that Christmas morning? • *A Northern Nativity*

Bill continued to paint his "message" pictures, but at first people most wanted paintings based on his prairie boyhood, often buying everything within minutes of a show opening.

His father saw him interviewed on television and admitted he'd made a mistake in wanting Bill to become a doctor or a teacher. "I had no idea then," he said, "what art was all about." It was his mother who worried that his success would not last. But it did.

He was invited everywhere as museums across Canada, the United States, and England showed his work. One Toronto show gave him special pleasure. He had painted the hardships of the Ukrainian settlers in Canada to honor his father. The wife of Canada's prime minister attended the opening and he was very proud indeed to introduce her to his parents.

It would be the first of his "immigrant" paintings. In a mural now in Canada's National Gallery, a Ukrainian child runs barefoot into the night snow, plate in hand, to beg for food. Women chop away tree stumps so the earth can be planted.

Would those settlers ever be able to clear all that forest to plant a farm? • *The Ukrainian Pioneer*

Bill went back to Alberta and Manitoba to paint where he had grown up. The shack where he was born was now a chicken coup. It was so small, he wondered how he could have been frightened at night when his parents' bed was so close to the one he had shared with his brother.

Because he knew the problems of his own parents, he wanted to paint the stories of all of Canada's minorities. He was able to complete six series: the Ukrainians, Jews, Poles, Irish, the French in Quebec, and the Inuit.

We see Jewish pioneers arriving at a prairie train station to settle on farms. He painted Polish men in Nova Scotia leaving a steel plant, while a mother and children stop to chat with the local priest. He traveled to the Far North twice to draw and paint the traditional life of the Inuit and how it was changing. In his Inuit Series, a mother chews animal skin to soften the leather for moccasins.

He dedicated his Irish Series to Jean, who helped him with the research. A particularly poignant painting was of a graveyard witnessing the deaths of so many who fled from famine in Ireland to die of typhoid fever in Canada.

A Quebec farm family enjoys a Sunday meal outdoors during Indian summer. • *They Sought a New World*

Immigrants had large families. Children were their faith in the future. Bill had six brothers and sisters. Though Bill wrote most about his father, it was his mother he painted, always showing her at work: cleaning out the chicken coup, feeding the pigs, getting cows into the barn.

He'd heard his parents tell of one summer when he was an infant and his father was too ill to work. "He had to look after me as best he could while Mother was out working the land with horses. . . . At the time she was probably pregnant with John."

His paintings show how pioneer women held families together. Food was important in keeping traditions of the countries they had left, particularly for holiday feasts and weddings. He painted himself looking at the table set for the Ukrainian Christmas, with the three tiered bread and the candle in the middle.

Other paintings of immigrant women show them working alongside the men. A Polish woman, hammer raised, helps her blacksmith husband.

Daughters worked beside mothers, as sons worked with fathers.

A mother makes Old Country food, while the father works outside. • *They Sought a New World* 25

The more famous Bill became, the more he gave away. He had always been generous with his paintings, giving them to friends and relatives, donating them to raise funds for charities.

Now it was money he gave. He was troubled by the poverty in the world. While his family lived modestly, he supported charities in Korea, Vietnam, India, South America, and a foster child in Hong Kong. He bought the house next to his and turned it into a home for Third World students. To pay for it, he drove himself ever harder.

Exhibition after exhibition, murals in church after church, writing and illustrating book after book, Bill hated to turn down an offer. He worked eighteen-hour days, often without eating. He fasted to remind himself of the world's starving people. He was working himself to death.

The only time he rested were the few weeks each summer spent with Jean and the children at their farm – then, and on the Ukrainian holidays when they all gathered at his parents'.

But sometimes other work took him away from his art. Even that he managed to turn into a painting. We see him shoveling snow outside his house, while his children play. It was a big snowfall for Toronto, but nothing like what he had known on the Prairies.

Was he remembering those open fields where they could draw a huge circle for the game of fox and geese?
And snowdrifts so high they could dig two-story apartments into them?

Digging out after a very big snowstorm in Toronto. • *O Toronto*

Bill compared the Prairies to the ocean, which many artists have painted. But no one painted the Prairies as he did. He seemed to remember every day he worked, played, suffered, and dreamed there through the long pain of growing up, its "soil, sky, cloud, wind, grass, poplar bush, snow, and sun."

"There was a time," he wrote, "during my boyhood in Manitoba – I used to feel the call of the great, free, flat bogland to the east of our farm. I found myself walking or cycling out on it whenever freed from work. Even though my father didn't actually own a single foot of it, it still said to me, 'You and I belong to each other.'"

He painted the Prairies stretching on forever to meet even greater skies. Children played as tiny creatures in the vastness. Everything and everyone moved toward the horizon: plows, wagons, trucks, and people.

Even a cow path led there. *Who is the little girl walking on it?*

The dedication of his book *A Prairie Boy's Summer* reads:

> With love to my sister Nancy
> Who more than anyone else shared with me the surprise and
> wonder of the prairie seasons as a child
> Who has added to that surprise and wonder a sense of awe and
> love for the Creator of those wonders.

He died before he could fulfill his promise to paint her prairie girlhood as a companion book to his own.

Even the cows moved toward the distant horizon. • *Fields*

In his search to understand his roots, Bill wanted to know the village his father had come from in the Ukraine. The Soviet Union restricted such travel. He had been allowed to visit it once for only four hours. He wanted to return to paint it.

In a last letter to a friend, he wrote, "I have been ill with something for the past half year. Nobody seems to know what's wrong. . . . It took eight years to get that special visa. That's why I'm going even if it kills me." He returned after three weeks with one hundred drawings and six paintings. When Jean and the children met him at the airport, they were shocked at how ill he looked. He would die six weeks later of cancer.

He was only fifty years old but he had achieved, he said, "success I never dreamed of." He left more than two thousand paintings, as well as murals and drawings, wrote and illustrated thirteen books, and had a marriage and family that gave him security.

Most important of all, he had broken free of his childhood problems.

While he was dying in hospital, his father visited him. Bill wanted to show him photographs he'd taken of his Ukrainian trip. His father, seeing how very sick he was, asked him to wait until he was feeling better.

Each was still trying to show how much he cared about the other.

The dam and pond at his father's village in the Ukraine "just as Dad remembered them."

William Kurelek's self-portrait. • *From a private collection*

William Kurelek

1927 Born in Whitford, Alberta

1934 Moved to Stonewall, Manitoba

1949 Graduated with a B. A. from the University of Manitoba

1949 Attended the Ontario College of Art, Toronto

1950 Attended the San Miguel Allende Art Institute, Mexico

1952 – 1959 Lived in England

1959 Returned to Canada. Settled permanently in Toronto.

1962 Married Jean Andrews. They had four children: Catherine, Stephen, Barbara, Thomas.

1977 Died in Toronto

Illustrations from his children's books, all published by Tundra Books:

A Prairie Boy's Winter 1973: Front Cover, Title Page, Pages 8, 9, 26

Lumberjack 1974: Pages 10, 11

A Prairie Boy's Summer 1975 (series now in the Windsor Art Gallery): Pages 4, 5, 6, 7

A Northern Nativity 1976: Pages 18, 19

They Sought a New World by Margaret S. Engelhart 1985: Pages 22 (left), 23, 24 (left), 25, Back Cover

Fox Mykyta by Ivan Franko, English version by Bohdan Melnyk 1978: Copyright Page

His adult art books published by Tundra Books:

Fields 1976: Pages 28, 29

The Polish Canadians 1981 (series now in the Hamilton Art Gallery)

To My Father's Village 1988: Page 30

Other illustrations are from:

The Niagara Falls Art Gallery: Page 13, From the series The Passion of Christ, 1960-63, Mathew 26: 18, Gouache and pencil
   on paper, 53.3 x 50.8 cm. Gift of Olha and Mykola Kolankiwsky. Permanent Collection: Niagara Falls Art Gallery –
   William Kurelek Collection. Pages 20 (top and bottom–detail), 21, From *The Ukrainian Pioneer* 1980, published by The
   Niagara Falls Art Gallery. Mural now in The National Gallery, Ottawa.

Kurelek's Canada 1975: Pages 16, 17, 24 (right) and *The Last of the Arctic* 1976, Pagurian: Page 22 (right)

Jewish Life in Canada 1976, Hurtig

O Toronto 1973, General: Page 27

Kurelek's Vision of Canada touring exhibition organized by Joan Murray, catalogue published by the Robert McLaughlin Gallery,
   Ottawa 1982 and by Hurtig 1983: Page 15

   Drawings and most of the quotes come from his autobiography *Someone with Me* (published by the psychology department
of Cornell University, 1973): Pages 3, 12, 14 (right). An abridged version without the drawings was published by McClelland &
Stewart, 1980. A complete version was issued by The Niagara Falls Art Gallery, 1988.

   The most detailed biography is *Kurelek* by Patricia Morley, Macmillan, 1986.

   William Kurelek's art is represented by Av Isaacs, P.O. Box 84, Toronto, Ontario M5V 3A8: Pages 14 (left), 15, 31